TO

LIST

To-Do List

Date:

Priority

To-Do List

Date:

Priority

To-Do List

Date:

Priority

To-Do List

Date:

Priority

To-Do List

Date:

Priority

To-Do List

Date:

Priority

To-Do List

Date:

Priority

To-Do List

Date:

Priority

To-Do List

Date:

Priority

To-Do List

Date:

Priority

To-Do List

Date:

Priority

To-Do List

Date:

Priority

To-Do List

Date:

Priority

To-Do List

Date:

Priority

To-Do List

Date:

Priority

To-Do List

Date:

Priority

To-Do List

Date:

Priority

To-Do List

Date:

Priority

To-Do List

Date:

Priority

To-Do List

Date:

Priority

To-Do List

Date:

Priority

To-Do List

Date:

Priority

To-Do List

Date:

Priority

To-Do List

Date:

Priority

To-Do List

Date:

Priority

To-Do List

Date:

Priority

To-Do List

Date:

Priority

To-Do List

Date:

Priority

To-Do List

Date:

Priority

To-Do List

Date:

Priority

To-Do List

Date:

Priority

To-Do List

Date:

Priority

To-Do List

Date:

Priority

To-Do List

Date:

Priority

To-Do List

Date:

Priority

To-Do List

Date:

>
>
>
>
>
>
>
>
>

Priority

>
>
>
>

To-Do List

Date:

Priority

To-Do List

Date:

Priority

To-Do List

Date:

Priority

To-Do List

Date:

Priority

To-Do List

Date:

Priority

To-Do List

Date:

Priority

To-Do List

Date:

Priority

To-Do List

Date:

Priority

To-Do List

Date:

Priority

To-Do List

Date:

Priority

To-Do List

Date:

Priority

To-Do List

Date:

Priority

To-Do List

Date:

Priority

To-Do List

Date:

Priority

To-Do List

Date:

Priority

To-Do List

Date:

Priority

To-Do List

Date:

Priority

To-Do List

Date:

Priority

To-Do List

Date:

Priority

To-Do List

Date:

Priority

To-Do List

Date:

Priority

To-Do List

Date:

Priority

To-Do List

Date:

Priority

To-Do List

Date:

Priority

To-Do List

Date:

Priority

To-Do List

Date:

Priority

To-Do List

Date:

Priority

To-Do List

Date:

Priority

To-Do List

Date:

Priority

To-Do List

Date:

Priority

To-Do List

Date:

Priority

To-Do List

Date:

Priority

To-Do List

Date:

Priority

To-Do List

Date:

Priority

To-Do List

Date:

Priority

To-Do List

Date:

Priority

To-Do List

Date:

Priority

To-Do List

Date:

Priority

To-Do List

Date:

Priority

To-Do List

Date:

Priority

To-Do List

Date:

Priority

To-Do List

Date:

Priority

To-Do List

Date:

Priority

To-Do List

Date:

Priority

To-Do List

Date:

Priority

To-Do List

Date:

Priority

To-Do List

Date:

Priority

To-Do List

Date:

Priority

To-Do List

Date:

Priority

To-Do List

Date:

Priority

To-Do List

Date:

Priority

To-Do List

Date:

Priority

To-Do List

Date:

Priority

To-Do List

Date:

Priority

To-Do List

Date:

Priority

To-Do List

Date:

Priority

To-Do List

Date:

Priority

To-Do List

Date:

Priority

To-Do List

Date:

Priority

To-Do List

Date:

Priority

To-Do List

Date:

Priority

To-Do List

Date:

Priority

To-Do List

Date:

Priority

To-Do List

Date:

Priority

To-Do List

Date:

>
>
>
>
>
>
>
>
>

Priority

>
>
>
>

To-Do List

Date:

Priority

To-Do List

Date:

Priority

To-Do List

Date:

Priority

To-Do List

Date:

Priority

To-Do List

Date:

Priority

To-Do List

Date:

Priority

To-Do List

Date:

Priority

Made in the USA
Monee, IL
27 December 2022

23489762R00065